KNEADING PEACE

What Sourdough Bread Taught Me
About Peacebuilding

Jenn Weidman

ISBN 979-8-218-81576-9

Book cover design by Soonthornwat (Shane) Wykoff.

Contents

For the bread bakers, the peacebuilders,
the critical yeast, and Kalil.

1. Introduction

How I Got Here

When I first read John Paul Lederach's *The Moral Imagination*, it felt as if the words were speaking to my soul. I was about 10 years into my work as a peacebuilder and the concepts in the book echoed exactly, and expanded on, what I was finding in my practice. *The Moral Imagination* rocked my world. It confirmed my own experiences and showed me how much more I was missing. On top of that, it gave me a framework through which to better conceptualize and think about what I was doing.

Now over 20 years into my peacebuilding work, that framework has stayed with me, holding true and bearing up under the spotlight of constant learning. Along the way, I've found a deepening of understanding, some of which is already included in *The Moral Imagination*, and some of which is adjacent to it. It's these insights that make up the heart of this book.

But first, we need to talk about bread.

Sourdough

When I say we need to talk about bread, I mean sourdough bread. Specifically, baking artisanal sourdough bread loaves.

I've written about how I got into baking sourdough bread before. I never set out to be a sourdough bread baker.

Like many people, a dear friend of mine began baking sourdough bread during the Covid-19 pandemic after her friend got her started. It was actually great for me since she would often deliver an extra loaf to me on baking day, still warm. I enjoyed listening to her talk about her sourdough journey, and of course, I loved eating her bread.

And then she got a new job in another country halfway around the world. Before she left she showed up at my door holding sourdough baking supplies and a jar containing her sourdough starter.

"This is Kalil. He's yours now."

That was when I discovered that when someone knocks on your door and gifts you their sourdough starter, you graciously accept and then just give in and take the plunge.

Becoming a sourdough bread baker took a bit of extra preparation for me. I live in Bangkok where ovens are not usually a feature of most apartments. When Kalil arrived on my doorstep, I had a small countertop oven that sufficed for daily use and casual baking. To continue my sourdough journey, however, I would need a full size proper oven that was large enough and could handle the higher temperatures required.

After a couple of months, a new oven, and a lot of videos about sourdough bread baking, I baked my first loaves. My friend named her sourdough starter Kalil when she gave him to me. She said, "Kalil means good friend, companion." And she was right. As I baked loaf after loaf, refining my skill, Kalil was my constant friend and companion. He still is.

When I work from home, he often sits, rising, next to me as I work. And approximately once a week we make bread together. He's started making appearances via pre-recorded videos in my classroom when I teach and I was gratified by one student, also a sourdough baker, who expressed deep concern for Kalil's health while I was away teaching for two weeks.

Because I live in the tropics, Kalil spends his down time chilling in the refrigerator. He ventures out for regular feedings and to make bread. In fact, he's sitting next to me right now and there will be bread tomorrow.

I started writing this book on Kalil's fifth birthday. My friend had him for about one year and he's been with me ever since. We like to joke that Kalil never fails, which I've found to be true. I've shared bits of Kalil with other aspiring sourdough bakers, one of whom has named her resulting sourdough starter Hope.

Hope lives with a baker who has tried many times over the years to start making sourdough. She told me that every time she tried, it never worked and her starter died. When I gave her a bit of Kalil, she named her new starter Hope as she was feeling hopeful about this new attempt. It's been almost a year now as I'm writing this, and Hope and her baker are thriving. Kalil, and now Hope, never fail.

I've learned many things on my sourdough bread baking journey. Yet what I never expected to learn was more about peacebuilding. I'd already read and digested John Paul's concept of critical yeast as outlined in *The Moral Imagination* and I'd baked enough to understand how it works. Baking sourdough with Kalil, however, brought me to another level of understanding of critical yeast, which is why this book is all about the relationship between peacebuilding and sourdough bread baking.

Haiku

Even before Kalil arrived at my door and I began to explore the possibilities that lie in the simple ingredients needed for bread and the practice of mixing them effectively, I was already cultivating my creativity through poetry, particularly haiku and the magical art of expressing the complex simply. Haiku, after all, includes only three lines of five syllables, seven syllables, and then five syllables. Just seventeen total syllables in which to express the essence of human experience.

Five seven and five
Can lived life fit inside it?
See, that's the challenge

In *The Moral Imagination*, John Paul takes a chapter to talk beautifully about haiku, his experience writing poetry, and its implications for peacebuilding. Chapter 7 speaks to my soul. It is one of those chapters that requires regular re-reading to remind and spur me to push deeper.

It's simply complex
Building peace and bridging gaps
So find the haiku

John Paul is also the reason I'm a bit of a haiku addict. I'd never written haiku before 2015 when we wrote haiku at a peacebuilding retreat with John Paul. Once I wrote the first one, haiku seemed to flow everywhere and about anything. I would be living life minding my own business when suddenly a haiku would appear.

John Paul Lederach
Launches new haiku addicts
I am one of them

Some years later I was looking for a way to bring more mindfulness and noticing into my daily life, to slow down inside and soak in the magic moments of life. Perhaps unsurprisingly, I took inspiration from John Paul's experiment with writing a haiku a day for a year and challenged myself to do the same. As I write this I'm in the seventh year of this pursuit.

A haiku a day
Brings mindfulness into life
Every single time

These days I write with a frequency that Oliver Burkeman calls "dailyish", such that most days end with me having written a haiku. And every time I re-read Chapter 7 of *The Moral Imagination*, I'm inspired to explore this practice with more depth. To fully explore the noticing, awareness, and intention in finding the haiku moments in life. To fully grasp the complexity and emerge into the simplicity on the other side.

It feels rather like a loaf of bread: a quite commonplace occurrence effortlessly holding complexity within simplicity.

Slow things down to the
Speed of sourdough baking
See what emerges

Four Disciplines of Peacebuilding

In *The Moral Imagination*, John Paul lays out four disciplines of peacebuilding and tells wonderful stories in illustration. The four disciplines are:

- The centrality of relationships
- The practice of paradoxical curiosity
- Providing space for the creative act
- The willingness to risk

If ever there was a recipe for peacebuilding, perhaps this is the beginning. Throughout my work, I've seen many examples of these four disciplines embodied in the actions of peacebuilders around the world. I am including two peacebuilders' stories here.

The Assassin

The first story centers on a peace leader who is the leader of a peace movement in his locality. He was born into a conflict zone that has seen an unresolved conflict brewing hot and warm but never cold for decades. He's simply the next generation inheriting the struggle. While there's a violent struggle where he lives, he and his movement have instead chosen to use nonviolent methods. As they gained recognition, he became a threatening figure to some other parties on various sides of the conflict. And they sent an assassin. This is the story of what happened next.

When the assassin came, he arrived at the peacebuilder's house and knocked on the door. The peace leader answered and knew full well who was at his door.

"Hello, welcome. Would you like to sit on my porch and have some tea?"

The assassin accepted the invitation and took a seat on the porch while the peace leader made them both tea. Serving the tea, he sat with the assassin and casually began a conversation while they sipped their tea.

An hour later, the assassin looked at the peace leader and said, "Yeah, I can't do this", and took his leave.

The invitation: paradoxical curiosity.
Tea on the porch: providing space for the creative act, the willingness to risk.
The conversation: the centrality of relationships.

Coffee & Relationships

The second story centers on another peacebuilder from the same place and a similar background. This peacebuilder is involved in the same movement as the peace leader who served the tea, and is also a person of interest for the parties on the other side of the struggle. In this story, that means the military that has been deployed to the area for decades to try to win the conflict.

One of the tactics the military regularly uses in this place is intimidation. To that end, they frequently send a group to visit the house of this peacebuilder. They come fully armed with an officer and some soldiers and knock on the peacebuilder's door.

Again, "Hello, would you like to sit on my porch and have some coffee?"

This peacebuilder loves slow drip coffee. The kind that you make fresh and slowly, beginning with grinding the beans by hand each time. He keeps his coffee-making kit in a bin that he can take with him anywhere he goes. While the officer and soldiers sit on the porch, he slowly, very slowly, makes coffee next to them.

Again, serving the coffee, he sits with them and casually starts a conversation. This scene plays out over and again, week on week, month on month.

The invitation: paradoxical curiosity.
Coffee on the porch: providing space for the creative act, the willingness to risk.
The conversation: the centrality of relationships.

One day, a skirmish happened between the armed side of the struggle and the military in which one young man from the community who was part of the armed struggle was killed. When his family came for his body to perform funeral rights according to their beliefs and culture, there was confusion about where his body was. The culture and beliefs in this place include a need for timely funeral rights and the stress on the family grew. After being bounced back and forth between the hospital and the military, the distressed and frustrated community did the only thing they could think of. The entire community began to walk down the road toward the military camp to retrieve the body of their son.

Halfway down the road, the military set up a road block with vehicles and soldiers. The community reached the road block and stopped. Our peacebuilder stood with other peacebuilding colleagues in between the community and the military and asked the community to sit down.

With the community seated in grief behind them, the peacebuilders faced the military, who were on alert, and asked for the body. Time passed. The lower ranking soldiers in the road didn't know anything and didn't have the authority to do anything. Frustrations rose. Tension built.

Eventually, after repeated requests from the peacebuilders to speak with the officer in charge, the officer came. The officer and the peacebuilder looked at each other with immediate recognition.

"It's you! Why didn't you tell them to tell me you were here?!"

"Sir, it's me. It's you. You know me. Can we please find resolution here?"

The relationship steadily built over many cups of slow coffee became the bridge.

The centrality of a relationship built though paradoxical curiosity, the creative act, and the willingness to risk bridged the gap and deescalated tensions, allowing space for resolution.

Food & Peace

In both of these stories, relationships were built around sharing food. Our friends shared tea and slow coffee. For the rest of the book, we'll be sharing bread.

The history of the interplay of food and peace is the history of humans. Like many others I've personally witnessed the power of sharing food to ground us, humanize the other, break barriers, bridge gaps, form connections, deepen relationships, and energize the weary.

While cooking, baking, and preparing food is not everyone's cup of tea, for me it's a creative outlet that grounds me, inspires me, and fuels my resilience. Spending time in the kitchen helps me create some space in my days to get out of my head and into my hands, to create and experiment, to slow down to the pace of food preparation, to take care and engage holistically with all my senses, and to nourish both myself and my household.

2. Critical Yeast &
How to Make Sourdough

Critical Mass & Critical Yeast

Before John Paul wrote about critical yeast, there was already a lot of conversation about critical mass: the concept of the amount of something needed to tip the balance. Critical mass has been used to answer questions like, "Do we have enough people?" Or, "How many people do we need to make this happen?" It's been applied to a wide variety of situations from referring to the proportion of people in a room in favor of a particular course of action, to the number of people needed to ensure the success of a nonviolent movement. As Erica Chenoweth and Maria Stephan write in their book, *Why Civil Resistance Works: The Strategic Logic of Nonviolent Conflict,* a nonviolent movement needs 3.5% of a population to be actively engaged to ensure its success. That's critical mass quantified.

While critical mass is important of course, John Paul's notion of critical, or strategic, yeast considers things from the other end of the spectrum and looks at the role of the smallest yet absolutely crucial part of the mix for change. In *The Moral Imagination*, John Paul lays out five principles for the role of critical yeast and how it works:

1. While the smallest ingredient in bread baking, yeast carries the potential for social change.
2. By itself, yeast has only potential without capacity.
3. At the start, yeast needs the right conditions and a safe, enabling environment to get going.
4. Yeast must be mixed in well and must be resilient enough to keep growing even after being knocked down.
5. The success of yeast requires attention to different things and processes that are happening at the same time and also coming up in the future; for example, preheating the oven at the appropriate time so everything is ready together.

As I continue to bake sourdough and work in peacebuilding and social change, I've found all of these principles to be true. And I've discovered a few more.

Note: Going forward in this book, when I talk about starter I'm referring to that magical mix of flour, water, and natural yeast critical to sourdough bread. When I mention critical yeast I mean the essential peace practitioners.

Making Sourdough

There are many ways to make sourdough bread. Every sourdough bread baker has their own method, techniques, tips, and goals. Some people strive for that picture perfect artisanal loaf with a very open, lacy crumb. Others prefer to bake sourdough in loaf pans so as to be easily sliced to fit well into a toaster and make classic lunchtime sandwiches. Some prefer a stronger sour taste to their loaves, while others focus on scoring their loaves in highly decorative and often themed designs. Approaches to help a baker achieve all of these goals fill shelves of books and countless webpages, social media groups, and classes and it can be daunting to find a place to begin.

Yet just beginning is actually the first key. The biggest learning in baking sourdough comes from the baking. It comes from the practice and experience of baking loaf after loaf, tweaking the process and ingredients here and there and noticing the impact on the results. An overload of information can keep prospective bakers paralyzed when the most useful thing they can do is just begin.

I find peacebuilding to be similar. While studying, learning, and preparing is important, sometimes we just need to start doing something. We need to begin small, practicing our skills and feeling our way around the process.

For me, when my friend knocked on my door and handed me Kalil, she also included some instructions and links to a few YouTube videos. Because I couldn't start immediately as I needed to acquire a better oven, which took a bit of time, I was able to ease into the flow of taking care of Kalil and explore some of the many suggestions out there for how to bake sourdough bread.

I first had to decide what kind of loaf I wanted. While pictures of lacy artisanal loaves captured my imagination, I wanted to be able to put things like cheese or jam on my bread without it falling through the holes. I wanted to be able to make sandwiches with my bread without the insides inconveniently leaking out. I also knew that the fact that I live in the tropics would impact the process and that some methods would not work well for me due to the heat and humidity.

Ultimately I decided to start by trying a method I learned in an online sourdough bread baking course that my household gifted to me. I expect the gift was both altruistic and self-serving, as helping me get over the line to start making bread meant both helping feed my new obsession and more imminent bread eating opportunities for my family.

The method I chose to begin with spans two days including a refrigerator stage, which works better for my tropical setting, and has a formula that is higher hydration (proportion of water to flour) than most bread, but still lower than many fancier or fussier sourdough formulations. Since I did not want that super open, lacy texture to my crumb, I didn't need to focus on super high hydration. Just enough would do. Also, starting with a slightly lower hydration mix is easier for the beginning sourdough baker.

My method also included some actual kneading in addition to the stretch and folds, and I like that. I like to get my hands in my dough and work with it. It gives me a closer understanding of what's happening inside the dough.

Don't worry if you're unfamiliar with these terms; clarity is coming. I also want to note that many volumes have been written on the science behind sourdough bread baking. And while I've read some of them and learned a lot, this book is in no way an attempt at a deep scientific explanation of the process.

Suffice it to say that making sourdough bread takes some hands on and hands in time alongside proportionately more waiting and patience, much like peacebuilding.

Sometimes to simply
Begin is the biggest block
To be overcome

Starter

The first key to sourdough bread baking is the starter. While many other yeasted breads use granulated yeast, either instant or otherwise, sourdough bread gets its rise from the starter. The starter isn't complicated. It is simply a mix of flour and water that contains natural, wild yeast. Where does it come from? Well, everywhere apparently. It is all around us and specific to locations, so the yeast you find in Kalil will be a bit different from the yeast you find in Hope because they live in different households, and more wildly different than the yeast you find in starters around the world.

Starters, like critical yeast, are locally contextualized and no two are the same. They often don't look like much from the outside, but they are brimming with potential. Inside an active starter, there is a lot going on. Starters are usually not flashy looking things. Instead, this critical yeast holds a deep connection with and understanding of the context.

To make sourdough bread, you must first ensure your starter is strong and active. Starters must be kept alive with regular feeding, which means adding flour and water in the right proportions to feed the yeast already in the mix and keep it happy. Feeding frequency for starters depends on the baker and how the starter is kept.

Kalil lives in the refrigerator because of the tropical climate where we live, so he can go longer between feedings. I feed Kalil approximately once a week and our routine seems to keep him happy and healthy. If you don't feed a starter, it can die when the yeast runs out of food.

I say approximately once a week because sometimes that doesn't happen, especially when I travel. The longest Kalil has gone without being fed was seven weeks. When I opened the lid of his jar to check in upon finally arriving home, he looked a little pitiful. But his spirit was still there and I fed him a couple times before we again made bread together.

Starters need to be nurtured with care, as a strong and healthy starter will give you the best bread. Critical yeast needs to be nurtured too, perhaps not as much with flour and water as with learning, confidence building, and skills. Critical yeast needs ongoing learning and growth. And unlike a sourdough starter, critical yeast often knows how to get these things for themselves. Sometimes they need support, and sometimes they don't. By listening carefully to what they're telling us, we can discover what both starters and critical yeast need.

People matter, and
We show up for each other
This is how we grow

Preparation

There is preparation I undertake every time before I make sourdough bread. The first is about scheduling. Because my method spans two days, I need to be sure I'll be home at the right times for the hands-on day, and again the following morning for the actual baking. While different methods allow for different levels of flexibility, the tropical climate and my limited fridge space pose additional challenges. Still, I found a method that works for me. What works for you may vary, and that's okay. There are many roads to good sourdough.

Once I've made sure the scheduling will work, I need to think about Kalil. Is he ready? Does he need to be fed a couple times before we make bread to get a bit stronger? Sometimes I feed him the day before starting to make bread, and other times I start making bread and feed him all at the same time. So before I start, I check in with Kalil and see how he's doing, what he needs, and what he's ready for.

Next, I make sure I have the ingredients I need. Since my sourdough loaves include only Kalil, water, a bit of salt, and flour, this usually means just checking that I have enough flour. I use a balanced mix of whole wheat flour, strong bread flour, and all purpose flour. I say a balanced mix because I've found that a key in getting the best bread is carefully balancing the proportions of strong bread flour and all purpose flour. The main difference between these two types of flours is the protein content and each brand will vary slightly. Yet even this slight variation will have significant impact on the texture and qualities of the finished loaves.

In the middle of my sourdough bread baking journey, I had to switch flours when different brands became unavailable or spiked in cost. This switch necessitated a rebalancing of the proportions of each. Thankfully, bread baking experiments are often edible, even if they have some room for improvement, and will make a perfectly fine toasted sandwich regardless.

With the timing checked, Kalil ready, and the other ingredients and supplies on hand, I can start making bread.

What is the preparation we undertake as we enter into peacebuilding work? What are the ingredients we use? Are we paying attention and carefully preparing the groundwork? Have we nurtured critical yeast? How do we know if everything is ready?

In many ways the preparation we do in peacebuilding centers around relationships between people and the groundwork is a web of connections. The mindsets, perspectives, and readiness of those in the web are essential to the preparation. Like with sourdough bread baking, part of the preparation is more logistical, part has to do with timing, and a key part is the readiness of the critical yeast.

Take care of yourself
Both the outside and inside
They go together

Levain

On the morning of the bread dough mixing day, I start by making a levain. A levain is sometimes called a preferment. Basically it's a mixture of Kalil, water, and flour that grows and then forms the basis of the dough. Essentially it is another feeding of Kalil, but I use different flour than during his normal meal.

To make the levain, I thoroughly mix some of Kalil with water and a balanced mix of strong bread flour and all purpose flour, making sure there are no lumps of flour.

Then I cover it and let the levain sit for somewhere from four to six hours and usually around the five-hour mark.

I check on it periodically and watch it growing, rising, and getting bubbly. There's a lot of activity that happens inside a levain. It is the first mix of the critical yeast with a small amount of other ingredients. This is where the power of the critical yeast begins to become apparent.

Growth

It always happens the same way whenever you feed a starter, whether an everyday feeding or if you're making a levain. You mix it together and let it sit and nothing happens.

One of the measures of the strength of a starter is how quickly it doubles in size once fed. A standard rule is that it should do that in four hours depending on the temperature. Kalil regularly meets this timeframe. He takes about four hours to reach the top of his jar when fed and the levain takes five hours on average.

But that four hours is not steady growth. Rather, the growth speeds up exponentially over time. I once took a time lapse video of Kalil after I fed him. The video was taken over a four-hour time span and I condensed it to 30 seconds. When I play it for people, they usually start by glancing at me wondering if I've actually pressed play yet. Nothing is happening on the screen. At five seconds in you can finally begin to see an ever so slight rise with the first tiny bubble appearing at seven seconds. And then at between 10 and 15 seconds into the video, it's as if the flood gates have opened as Kalil quickly rises, bubbling away, to the top of his jar. The vast majority of the growth happens in the last half of the time.

Peace and critical yeast are like that too. How many times do we see a nonviolent movement become successful seemingly in a relatively short period of time? The temptation is to assume that what we saw is all that happened. Yet that's never the case. Behind every successful "rising", there is decades of work, much of it hidden.

It is happening inside. If we're very observant and attuned, we can spot the first small bubble. And then it will seem to almost go dormant again, until the flood gates open and it really takes off.

When we're working with people we see as critical yeast, there will always be a period in which we think nothing is happening. This part needs patience. Because something is always happening, even if it is small or nearly invisible. We need to tune in closely to see the first bubble and then breathe with patience through the quiet work needed before the exponential growth.

Kalil proves the point
You see, critical yeast grows
Exponentially

When is the Levain Ready?

So how do you know when the levain is ready to use? Timings are guidelines only, since many factors impact the growth of the critical yeast. Heat, humidity, and the mojo of the starter on the day, just to name a few, will all impact how the levain grows. The best measure is careful observation.

The most common guidance for knowing when the levain is ready to use is to watch for it to peak. That means to watch for the moment when it has risen as high as it is going to rise and is just starting to fall.

While the yeast consumes the flour and water mixed into the levain, it will rise and bubble. When the food becomes mostly consumed, it will start to fall and deflate and get weaker. And a weak starter or levain doesn't make good bread.

You know your levain has hit its peak when you look at it, shake it a bit, and see a few bubbles burst on the surface. If you are looking carefully, you can actually see it start to fall, to collapse in on itself.

Common wisdom says a levain at its peak makes the best bread.

And yet, I'm not so sure.

At some point as I was poking around in various online resources about sourdough, I came across an approach that uses the levain just before it peaks when its momentum and growth energy are high. I found it an interesting proposition so I tried it. The next time I made bread I used the levain just before it peaked and the resulting loaves were some of my best ever.

As I thought more about it, I noticed parallels in peacebuilding as well.

As someone who started her earlier career path as always a bit too young for whatever I was doing at the time, I have a soft spot for brilliant younger people. Over and again in my work, I see the tension between colleagues across the age and experience spectrum.

During an event I was facilitating, I had a fascinating conversation with a participant over breakfast. He told me about his over 30 years of experience working in environmental law. He was one of the people with the foresight to know that the future would even more acutely need strong environmental law frameworks. His organization at the time was made up of a young team and he eagerly described his working philosophy like this:

> When a younger or newer person brings an idea, you always hear the more experienced people say some thing like, "No. It won't work. We tried it before." But that's not our job. Our job is not to discourage and just say no all the time. Our job is to say something like, "We tried that before and had these challenges. Do you think that will be a problem this time and how will you overcome

it?" The context changes. The people change. It is never the same thing twice. Just because something didn't work before doesn't mean that it won't work this time — that there's not a way to do it so that it will work.

Exactly.

The levain is ready to use just before it seems to be ready. Does it feel ready? Maybe not. It looks like it's still growing. And yet that's when it makes the best bread. Yes, the levain will benefit from the knowledge and experience of a veteran sourdough bread baker. And the veteran baker will see greater impacts and better bread from putting their trust in a young levain.

So, to people who don't feel quite ready yet, especially young people, don't wait. You'll never feel ready. So just begin. Do it anyway. Keep your eyes and ears wide open, learn along the way, seek input and wisdom from others, and then do it.

And to the people with decades of experience, it's time to share learnings, support those stepping up, and take a chance on a levain before its peak.

> Are you ready yet
> And does it really matter
> Time waits for no one

Your State of Mind Matters

One of the most unexpected things I learned about making sourdough bread is that your state of mind matters. While it seems crazy to think that my mood influences how my bread comes out, I've found it to be true. If I'm grumpy or anxious or angry, the bread never comes out as good.

So now when I start making bread, I check my mood and my state of mind. If I find it rather less than ideal for bread making, I intentionally slow down. We all know that it's hard, if not impossible, to will yourself to instantly change your mood. So I slow down and deepen my engagement with the dough. I notice more, I use my senses to connect with the dough and ground myself in it, regardless of which step in the process I'm working on. Soon enough, the dough and I have both found an even keel.

I've found that intention is essential. In life, in relationships, in sourdough baking, in peacebuilding. Intention and the attention that accompanies it hold the key to the difference between done and done well, checking things off a list and deep impact.

How do we approach our work? Do we bring appropriate intention and attention? As peacebuilders, what's the state of mind we carry throughout? Are we fatalistically skeptical? Do we carry hope, the unwavering belief that a better future is possible albeit difficult to achieve?

Peacebuilding is hard and it takes a long time. Sometimes we feel as though we are constantly losing to the unstoppable tide of violence, oppression, injustice, and more. Yet peace is always worth working for, regardless of the obstacles and challenges. So when we wake up to find the world falling apart again, it is time to get to work with renewed energy.

I've written about personal resilience elsewhere. Here, on our journey with critical yeast, I want to sit with this question:

What state of mind do we ourselves hold as we engage critical yeast, as we begin the mixing process, as we start exponential growth, as we work towards peace?

Any day's better
When you're making bread and it
Keeps you company

Mixing, Autolyse, & Kneading

When the levain is ready, full of growth momentum, and just before its peak, it's time to start mixing. At this point I use the autolyse method, which simply means I mix most of the ingredients and then let them sit together a bit before continuing.

The levain, more water, and a proper balance of bread flour, whole wheat flour, and all purpose flour, all go into a big bowl. At this stage I start mixing with my hands and squeezing everything through my fingers. It's essential to ensure things are well mixed and there are no lumps. It will look rough, but that's ok. Then I let it sit for about 20 minutes for the flours to hydrate well and everything to start gelling. This is the autolyse.

When critical yeast is mixed into the full dough, it can seem rough in the beginning and everything benefits from some time for everyone to get acquainted and established, to get their feet under them, if you will.

After 20 minutes, the rough mixture is already starting to pull together as a proper dough. At this point I mix in the final ingredient, salt. Adding the salt too early will kill the yeast and hinder growth. Yet without the salt the dough won't develop properly. I often use a bit more water just to help the salt dissolve well into the dough and to help everything to come together nicely.

Once the salt is well incorporated, it's time to knead. Kneading encourages gluten to form, which creates the texture of the bread and provides the scaffolding for the air bubbles that create the open crumb of good sourdough bread.

Because sourdough dough is wetter than other bread dough, different kneading techniques are needed. The first time I kneaded my dough it was quite a mess. With practice, I've gotten better at it and found my rhythm.

When do you know you've kneaded enough? You have to pay attention to the dough, how it looks and feels and behaves. Usually I let the dough rest for five minutes in the middle of the kneading. It's amazing the difference this short rest makes in the dough formation as it transforms from a shaggy mass to a smooth and coherent dough.

Kneading my dough often prompts me to think about being in the middle by being on the edge, a concept laid out by Steven and Sue Williams in their book, *Being in the Middle By Being At the Edge: Quaker Experience of Non-Official Political Mediation*. The concept of being in the middle by being on the edge is first mentioned in the book as a perspective, a way to be in the middle of conflict situations by being on the edge in how you perceive things and leaving yourself open to hearing and understanding all sides. It means taking the often unpopular stance in a conflict situation of not taking a side, but rather understanding all sides.

The book then goes on to explore more about the Quaker approach to mediation and how being in the middle by being on the edge can also be spatial and dynamic. How it can mean attending to efforts that may result in different parties coming together without you. Or how it can mean that you are ultimately not present when the culminatingly important things happen.

Steven and Sue summarize it well in the final paragraph of the main part of the book:

Unofficial mediators know that all they can do is to offer possibilities. It is for someone else to decide whether and in what form to take up those possibilities. And so the process comes full circle. We began by saying that the mediator stays in the middle by being always at the edge. In this sense as well, the mediator maintains a useful role in the middle, by being willing to be left outside the inner circle. Having moved to the middle in order to build relationships, processes, and connections, the mediator then moves willingly to the edge, to allow the participants to come together.

I relate strongly to this concept. And I find it rather like making bread, and kneading. While I'm obviously involved in the process and in many ways am in the middle, I'm not actually inside the dough. My actions influence the enabling environment that allows the gluten to form yeast to grow properly, but I don't control the process. That is part of both the joy and frustration of sourdough bread baking. The dough will always have a mind of its own and will be more or less cooperative each time. In the end, the dough will become bread while I stand on the edge doing the only thing I can do: watch and wait.

The watching and waiting actually comes and goes throughout the bread making process from the levain onwards. Like the five-minute rest in the middle of the kneading stage where I just let the dough do its thing, sitting on the bench, covered by an opaque bowl. I have no idea what is happening in there and don't know what it will look like until I remove the bowl for the final kneading, but I always trust that dough forces are at play and it will come out better than before the rest. And it always does.

What goes on outside
Affects what goes on inside
Also the reverse

Proving & Stretch & Folds

Once the dough is properly kneaded and has gotten a start on its development, it is time to pop it in a bowl and wait. I usually use a glass bowl for this so I can periodically cast an eye over in its direction and see how it's getting on.

Proving is an extended period of rest when the dough grows and develops. During this time it is important to ensure the dough is kept at an appropriate and constant temperature. A warmer temperature speeds up the proving time while a cooler temperature slows it down, allowing for more depth of flavor to develop. The right balance is important.

During proving, the dough will rise and increase in volume. Bubbles will form inside and may be visible on the outside as well.

There's not much to do during the proving stage except for a series of stretch and folds. Stretch and fold is a technique in which the dough is, well, stretched and folded in on itself. It helps the formation of the gluten in the dough.

Some bakers do this in the proving bowl. For me, I turn the dough out onto a lightly floured board, stretch it into a rough square or rectangle, and then fold it in thirds both directions, top and bottom and then left and right. Stretch and folds are always done quickly. Then it's back into the proving bowl.

The number of stretch and folds and the timing in between them vary by method. My method is relatively simple as I only do two stretch and folds about 45 minutes apart. Because I've already kneaded my dough, I don't need to do more. Some bakers don't knead their dough at all and encourage gluten formation primarily through a more intricate system of stretch and folds. There are many ways to make great bread.

Most of the proving stage is hands-off time for the baker. I set a timer and then do other things, casting a glance at the bowl of rising dough from time to time and intervening only if needed to keep the temperature relatively constant. The dough needs this distant monitoring and periodic, quick stretch and folds to maximize its potential, but the real work is all happening inside. It's important not to fuss with it too much at this stage and just let it do its thing. The baker is again mostly on the edge.

Just like there are many ways to make great bread, there are also many good approaches to peacebuilding. Some things they have in common are this no fuss phase, this period of distant monitoring with periodic hands-on moments to encourage the process.

It is ours to live
Loud and large, small and quiet
Just, with intention

When is it Properly Proved?

One of the biggest questions in all bread baking, including sourdough, is how to know if the dough is properly proved and ready for the next step in the process. Underproved dough will not have the strength to rise into a nice round loaf when baked and will be gummy when cut. Overproved dough will also not have the strength for a big rise when baked. It will collapse on itself as it tries to rise, rather like how overworked leg muscles refuse to work properly if tested again too soon after a hard leg workout. And the trick is that you often won't really know for sure until the bread is baked.

Time alone is often an unreliable indicator as variations in temperature and humidity can extend or shorten timelines, so many bakers also pay attention to volume. Yet, not surprisingly, there are different ideas about how much volume gain indicates properly proved sourdough. Some guidelines state the dough should have doubled in size while I've seen others swear by an only 50 percent rise in volume.

And there are other indicators aside from time and volume. You can find hours of video and countless pages in books and online trying to help bakers pinpoint the exact perfect moment to end the proving. In addition to tracking time and change in volume, you may smell the dough, jiggle it looking for the appropriate wobble, and press a finger into it looking for the dough to bounce back in just the right amount of time — not too fast and not too slow.

Knowing when the dough is properly proved is a pivotal and crucial step. If you want a glimpse into the seriousness of this determination, just tune into an episode of *The Great British Bake Off* during bread week. You will see bakers collapse into puddles of indecision and hear Paul Hollywood comment again and again on the proving of each loaf he tastes.

When is the dough ready? Or when is a movement or peacebuilding process ready for the next step? In the end, intuition, experience, and being in tune with your dough and the work of the critical yeast are again the keys.

Step in or step back
Do what you need to do, yet
Know which is hard

Preshaping & Shaping

Once you've finally determined that the time is right to move on from the proving stage, it's time to shape the loaves. I usually make two, large round loaves, or boule, from one batch of sourdough. While shaping isn't inherently difficult, it is rather particular.

First I tip my dough out of its proving bowl onto a lightly floured surface. Then I divide it into as many loaves as I want to make with swift and decisive cuts of a bench scraper. Each loaf is then preshaped. This means gently but intentionally pulling pieces from the edges into the middle to create a sort of upside down loaf shape. Preshaping needs to be done a bit gently and with intention so as to not knock all the air out of the dough yet still be effective. Each pre-shaped loaf is then covered and left to rest for another 20 minutes.

While this rest can feel like a false start, it isn't. Preshaping seems simple but it is an important and fundamental shift from dough that's proving to loaves in process, from a lot of talk and laying the groundwork to really coming together around an agreement in process. The resting time after preshaping is indicative of a fundamental principle of both bread baking and peacebuilding: don't rush the process.

During the resting time I prepare the next set of equipment that I need. My sourdough method includes a fridge stage during which my shaped loaves spend the night snugly chilling in the fridge. This slows down fermentation while allowing more time for flavor to develop. Not every baker does this. If you're baking in cooler climates, you may just extend the bulk fermentation, or proving, stage. In the tropics, that's never really an option for me if I want flavorful bread.

While not all bakers rest their loaves in the fridge, sourdough bread usually spends some time in a basket called a baneton before being baked. Banetons are proving baskets made from rattan that can help loaves hold different shapes. Some bakers use them as is and the rattan cane imprints patterns into the tops of the loaves. I use a muslin liner in mine. Either way, the baneton or the liner must first be dusted with flour to ensure the dough doesn't stick.

I only have two banetons. So when I want to make smaller loaves to use as bread bowls for soup or individual servings of cheese fondue, for example, I have to improvise. A bowl or large muffin tin lined with a tea towel dusted with flour works just fine too. There is always space for improvisation in bread baking and peacebuilding.

Moments of breakthrough in peacebuilding often happen during improvisation as peacebuilders take advantage of the right place and time to adjust and adapt to surroundings, changing contexts, cultures, and the flow of dialogue. Some of the most impactful conversations can happen in unplanned places — while taking a stroll, in an air raid shelter, while taking a quick rest on a bench or under a tree, or huddled unexpectedly in the corner of a hotel lobby after a chance meeting. It often happens outside the more official structures; we don't have to only use banetons.

Once the preshaped loaves have rested, it's time for the final shaping. There are many ways and shapes in which to form the dough. I usually make big round loaves. One at a time and again gently and with intention, I repeat the preshaping and then flip the loaf over and repeatedly pull it toward me, my fingers slightly cupped underneath. The key is to create tension over the top surface of the loaf and ensure the bottom is sealed. The tension is critical. Without this surface tension, the loaf will not spring up with a big rise when baked in the oven.

Sometimes I need to remind myself that tension can be constructive and even necessary for growth in life as well.

While society continues to encourage us to avoid all sorts of discomfort and tension, I find this creative tension essential to breakthroughs. Creative tension, not heat. At this stage in my sourdough bread baking process, it is important to control and even lessen the temperature to allow deep flavor to develop. In peacebuilding, we have to know how to take the heat out of the situation to allow the energy of creative tension to be used for problem solving.

Shifting transitions
Can also be beautiful
It is up to you

Fridge Stage

Once I've got it properly shaped, I pop the shaped loaves upside down into the prepared banetons, wrap the whole thing in a bag to keep it from drying out, and rush it into the fridge. My tropical climate means that I'm more prone to overproving than underproving my loaves so I'm usually looking to get them into the fridge quickly to slow down the fermentation process.

With all the loaves I'm making safely tucked into the fridge, I usually announce to my household that the fridge door is to be opened and shut minimally and quickly. If the fridge isn't cool enough or the temperature varies too much, I risk my loaves overproving overnight. Some years ago this is actually the way I knew our refrigerator was malfunctioning and not holding its temperature!

There's not much more to say about the fridge stage. The only thing I need to do is leave it be, not interfere with the fridge environment too much, and get a good night's sleep. Both bakers and peacebuilders need good rest.

So good night moon and
Cooking spoons. Good night haiku
And good night to you

Heating the Oven & Equipment

Since I know I'll bake the loaves the morning after popping them into the fridge and I know that I wake up earlier than my household, I usually prepare my baking setup before going to bed so as to not make too much noise in the morning. Here's what I prepare:

- Oven rack on the bottom rack
- Additional oven racks removed because I need the space
- Baking stone on the oven rack in the oven
- Large cast iron pot with lid on the baking stone in the oven
- Parchment paper ready
- Lame (scoring tool) ready
- Heavy duty oven gloves ready
- Cooling rack ready

While you can innovate some supplies, for other items the right equipment is necessary.

Sourdough loaves are usually baked in a steamy environment to form that signature crispy crust. While some bakers open bake in the oven and then need to make sure to add steam into their oven, I bake in a large cast iron pot with the lid on. The smaller enclosed space means that the steam that escapes from the dough during the baking process is enough to form a nice crust.

Heavy duty oven gloves are a must. Sourdough is usually baked at very high temperatures and the cast iron pot will be scorching hot. Protection is important!

With everything prepared and my loaves chilling, I go to sleep. The following morning, I wake up and immediately turn the oven on to full blast, the highest temperature it can reach, which for my oven is about 250C. I go about my morning while the oven with the baking stone and pot inside all preheat for about an hour. To ensure the baking stone and pot are fully heated, the oven needs to preheat beyond when the temperature indicator shows it is ready.

While you might assume that preheating the oven is something all sourdough bakers do, there are, unsurprisingly, many approaches to baking temperatures and methods. Some sourdough bakers swear by a cold start method that does not require any preheating of the oven. Others prefer a super hot start and then turn down the heat immediately once the bread is in the oven. Again, whatever works for you, works.

In the midst of the many opinions on the "right" way or "best" way to bake sourdough bread, for me it's important to keep the goal in sight. The goal is good bread, not proving that any one bread baking, or peacebuilding, method is the definitive right and best way. It's all about the bread, and the peace.

How do you process
All that could have been and what
Actually was

Scoring

Once the oven with the baking stone and pot inside is fully heated, it is finally time to bake!

I cut a square of parchment paper and retrieve a loaf from the fridge. After tipping it out from the baneton onto the parchment, I score the top of the loaf. Scoring is cutting slashes into the dough so that when it bakes it has more space to rise and bake up into a nicely shaped loaf instead of busting out of its crust in strange places. I use a lame for this, a razor attached to a handle, but a super sharp knife also works. It just needs to be very sharp.

Every baker has their own scoring pattern that works for them and some get highly decorative with their scoring, creating themed patterns and decorations. I don't get that fancy. Still, scoring can be like a baking fingerprint and I'd know my loaves anywhere because of it. I always make the same cuts and so my loaves always bake up looking a certain way. This may be where peacebuilding and bread making diverge a bit, as no two peacebuilding processes progress the same even if the same peacebuilders are involved.

Baking

After scoring the loaf, I take the pot out of the oven and pop the loaf inside, using the corners of the parchment paper to help lift it in. Then it's quickly into the oven, still at full heat, with the lid on for 25 minutes. For the first part of my bake I can't even see how it's going since my pot is opaque.

When my timer rings, I'm always eager to take the pot out of the oven, lift the lid, and see how the bread is shaping up. My bread spends the final 15 minutes of its bake sitting directly on the baking stone and getting a nice, crispy, caramelized crust at an ever so slightly cooler oven temperature.

Baking is the ultimate moment of being on the outside and letting go. I've done absolutely everything I could do to support good loaves. Now it's up to them. The time has come to fully step back and trust in the critical yeast and all the work that has led to this point. In the end, the baker, and the peacebuilder, must let go.

Accepting things you
Can no longer change though you've
Changed them in the past

Eating

When the bread is fully baked and golden, it sits on a rack to cool. This may be one of the most difficult parts of the entire process — the waiting at the end. While it smells and looks absolutely delicious, you must wait. Cutting a sourdough loaf while still warm can turn your lovely crumb to a gummy texture and stunt its flavor. While the loaf cools, some of the flavor from the caramelized crust gets pulled into the bread, giving the final nuance to its taste.

And so we wait and keep our hands off while the loaf solidifies itself entirely without our intervention.

And then, finally, it is time to eat, to celebrate!

There's nothing quite like that first piece of fresh bread. The sound the knife makes cutting through the crust and the feel of the knife moving through the loaf is a beautiful symphony of the senses.

As you eat the bread, plain or with whatever toppings or dips you prefer, it's truly a precious moment. Your sole focus is on the taste and texture and the full experience of eating. The yeast is forgotten. The process is in the past. The patience, intention, attention, and care are rewarded. Everything is subsumed into this delicious point in time so that now there is only this beautiful bread.

Many peacebuilders have used the analogy of peacebuilding being like a bridge, making connections. And bridges are made to be walked over. If, as a peacebuilder, your work is forgotten as the parties move forward together toward a better future, then that is success. It is all about the bread, after all. And Kalil watches from his spot in the fridge as the bread he fueled is enjoyed, waiting to make the next loaves.

Endings are also
Beginnings dressed up well in
Different colored clothes

3. Conclusion

So where does this leave us, aside from blissfully enjoying fresh bread?

We started with John Paul's four disciplines of peacebuilding and five principles of critical yeast. Here I would add a few more principles of critical yeast.

First, Kalil, and Hope, never fail. Throughout any peacebuilding process we need the accompaniment of a good friend and companion. And we need to walk with hope, the unwavering belief that a better future is possible. Not easy, possible.

I often recall Elise Boulding's concept of hope and vision in which she would say: "If you can't dream it, you can't have it." If the kind of sourdough loaf you want is not clear to you, if you do not have the vision of it, if you can't see it in your mind's eye, then you will never be able to bake it.

We need to hold the vision, walking with hope, accompanied by a good friend and companion.

Second, critical yeast grows exponentially both in volume and in time. In the beginning it will seem like nothing is happening when, in fact, the internal and often invisible groundwork is being laid for unstoppable, exponential growth. We need to be patient, notice deeply, and pay close attention to see the signs.

Third, critical yeast is best before it is ready, before it reaches its peak. While the temptation is to wait until people feel ready, we may never feel ready and the best results often come from starting just before that, when growth and energy are high. Instead of waiting for a sometimes elusive peak moment, we should move forward before that with intention, attention, adaptation, constant learning, and lessons from experience beyond our own.

Fourth, much of the process of peacebuilding requires us to be in the middle by being on the edge in different ways in both perspective and space. Working with critical yeast by its very nature means that at some point we will be left out of the inner circle and will be on the edge when the bread is finally baked.

Fifth, while the process may be long and nuanced, it is always well worth the effort. Even when things don't go perfectly, the bread is still edible and lessons are learned and applied moving forward. While the sourdough bread baking process seems complicated, it's now second nature to me. Long and nuanced peacebuilding processes seem more achievable the more we engage with them. And the more bread we bake, the better the loaves.

Sixth, bridges are made to be walked over and in the end, it's all about the bread, or the peace. While we can learn from different perspectives and experiences, the goal is still good bread, not a definitive declaration of the right or best process or claiming credit or ownership. There are many ways to make good sourdough bread. And in the end if people forget the baker or the peacebuilder while enjoying their delicious bread and the peace, then that is success.

In the end, what could be seemingly simpler than a loaf of bread — a simple, everyday item. Yet this loaf, this peace, is the culmination of a nuanced process of mixing and baking and holds the full complexity of generations of human skill, learning, and knowledge about working with flour, water, salt, and critical yeast.

> Five seven and five
> The soul of peacebuilding both
> Simple and complex

A Recipe for Peacebuilding, Now

At the end of *The Moral Imagination*, John Paul includes a poem that is a good recipe for peace.

Reach out to those you fear.
Touch the heart of complexity.
Imagine beyond what is seen.
Risk vulnerability one step at a time.

You will never feel ready. Don't wait. Just do something, no matter how small. Start now.

If you're on your way as a peacebuilder, check your critical yeast. Is it nourished and ready? If not, feed it. It is time to rise.

My Sourdough Formula & Method

If you are inspired to make sourdough bread, here's the way I do it and my formula.

Day 1:

Levain:

227g warm water
45g sourdough starter
127g all purpose flour*
100g bread flour*

* You may need to adjust this balance depending on the protein content of your flour. The recipe calls for all 227g of flour to be bread flour but that didn't work as well for me.

Put starter then water then flour(s) in a bowl. Combine and mix until smooth. Cover and allow to ferment in a warm place for some hours. It could be 4 to 6 to 8 hours depending on the temperature, etc. The levain is ready when it has risen, is bubbly, and is just about to fall, or ideally right before this.

Autolyse:

400g water (I withhold 50g to use later, which seems to work better in my tropical climate)
254g bread flour*

200g all purpose flour*
All the levain minus 45g
228g whole wheat flour
17g salt (added after autolyse)

* You may need to adjust this balance depending on the protein content of your flour. The recipe calls for all 454g of flour to be bread flour but that didn't work as well for me.

Remove 45g of levain from the levain — I put this back in my starter jar. Add levain then 350g water then flours to a bowl but hold back the salt. Note: I never weigh the levain at this stage; I just take out the 45g and use the rest. Mix by hand until thoroughly incorporated and homogenous. The dough will be shaggy. Cover and allow to autolyse for 20 minutes.

After the autolyse, add the salt into the bowl and mix with your hands and a dough scraper in the bowl to incorporate. I use some of the reserved water to help this process along.

Turn the dough out of the bowl and knead by hand until it is smooth and ready, incorporating a 5-minute kneading intermission in the middle of the kneading process. I mostly use a combination of three methods: slap and flip, squeezing, and cutting. You can wet your hands in any leftover reserved water to help it not stick if needed.

Place the dough into a container with a lid and allow to ferment for 45 minutes.

Fold 1: Turn dough out onto a lightly floured surface. Stretch it out a bit, then fold the top third down, bottom third up, right third over, left third over. If the dough is a bit too sticky, dust your hands with flour before folding.

Return dough to the container, cover with the lid, and allow to ferment for 45 minutes.

Fold 2: Repeat the folding process.

Return dough to the container, cover with the lid, and allow to ferment for 45 minutes or longer until the dough is ready.

When dough is ready, turn it out onto a lightly floured surface and divide into two pieces. Preshape each piece into a loose, round ball, and place bottom up on a lightly floured surface. Cover the loaves and allow them to rest for about 20 minutes.

Shape the loaves into boules and place them seam-side up in a well-floured proofing basket. I use all purpose flour for this. Place the proofing basket in a plastic bag and tie the bag, or cover with a shower cap. Place in the fridge overnight.

Day 2:

Place a baking stone and cast iron Dutch oven with the lid in the oven with the Dutch oven sitting directly on the baking stone. Preheat the oven to as hot as it can go, which for me is about 250C, for an hour.

When ready, invert a proofing basket onto a square of parchment paper, dumping the loaf out. Gently smooth out the flour on top of the boule. Score the boule. As quickly as possible, pop the boule into the Dutch oven, using the parchment paper to lift it in, and cover with the lid. Quickly place the Dutch oven back into the oven on top of the baking stone and bake for 25 minutes.

After 25 minutes, pull the Dutch oven out of the oven, gently remove the loaf, place it directly on the baking stone, and continue baking for another 15 minutes. You can lessen the oven temperature a titch so the loaf doesn't get too dark in color.

Remove loaf and cool completely on a rack. Place the Dutch oven with the lid on back into the oven for at least 15 minutes to preheat a second time before repeating the baking process with the second loaf.

Allow loaves to cool completely before slicing.

Resources that Influenced My Thinking

The Moral Imagination, by John Paul Lederach

Why Civil Resistance Works: The Strategic Logic of Nonviolent Conflict, by Erica Chenoweth and Maria Stephan

Being in the Middle By Being At the Edge: Quaker Experience of Non-Official Political Mediation, by Steven and Sue Williams

Elise Boulding

Homemade Sourdough from Starter to Baked Loaf with Richard Miscovich, Craftsy Class

Tartine Bread, by Chad Robertson

Sourdough Geeks Facebook Group

Acknowledgements

This book would not have been possible without the inspiration and support of so many. I can't name everyone, but let me make a start. I want to thank:

John Paul Lederach for being himself, writing *The Moral Imagination*, inspiring me, and mentoring me through some key moments.

Kalil and Ivanka, my dear friend and Kalil's first baker.

My mom, who gifted me the sourdough bread baking class that kicked it all off and who eagerly waited to tuck in to the ends of each loaf that followed.

Peacebuilders and colleagues who inspire me: Chaiwat, Charlie, Emma, Emmanuel, Herm, Irene, Jan, Mark, Michael, Miki, Moh & Pearl, Nikki, Numfundo, Sunny, Tania, Tom, colleagues at ALLMEP, colleagues in Myanmar, colleagues in Thailand, colleagues in Ukraine, and many others.

My students, who helped me refine these concepts through class discussions.

Michael, who came back to help me edit another book. Your input is always absolutely invaluable.

Shane, who visually captured the essence of things.

About the Author

In addition to baking sourdough bread, Jenn is a process facilitator and peacebuilder, building resilience into leadership development for the organizations and teams working to solve the world's most intractable problems. She is founder and CEO of Space Bangkok, a social enterprise based in Bangkok, Thailand, that works globally to support peacebuilding, resilience, trauma informed practice, leadership development, and strategic problem solving using creative facilitation, capacity building, and accompaniment.

Want to continue the conversation?

Find Jenn on LinkedIn: www.linkedin.com/in/jenn-weidman/

www.ingramcontent.com/pod-product-compliance
Lightning Source LLC
Chambersburg PA
CBHW060521280326
41933CB00014B/3049